I0569353

SIMONE WILLIAMS YOUNG

After the Anointing Lifts

Who Are You?

First published by Young at Heart Publishing LLC 2024

Copyright © 2024 by Simone Williams Young

All rights reserved. No part of this publication may be reproduced, stored or transmitted in any form or by any means, electronic, mechanical, photocopying, recording, scanning, or otherwise without written permission from the publisher. It is illegal to copy this book, post it to a website, or distribute it by any other means without permission.

First edition

ISBN: 979-8-9898143-3-6

This book was professionally typeset on Reedsy.
Find out more at reedsy.com

"that he might present it to himself a glorious church, not having spot, or wrinkle, or any such thing; but that it should be holy and without blemish."

EPHESIANS 5:27 KJV

Contents

Preface

~~~~~~~~

When the Anointing Lifts: Who Are You?

Discovering True Identity Beyond the Mantle

We often marvel at those who operate under the anointing of God. They shine brightly, their gifts captivating and drawing people in. Yet, a crucial question lingers: who are we when the anointing lifts? This book seeks to explore the essence of our true selves beyond the mantle we carry. It challenges us to examine our integrity, our everyday lives, and our alignment with the fruits of the Spirit.

In my journey as an author, walking with the Lord, and leadership in ministry, I have seen and encountered many individuals who grapple with their identity once the anointing lifts. The moments of powerful ministry and supernatural experiences are exhilarating, but what happens when those moments fade? How do we navigate the quiet seasons, the ordinary days, and the challenges that test our character?

This book is an invitation to embark on a journey of self-discovery and spiritual growth. It's about peeling back the layers and understanding who we are at our core, beyond the spiritual highs. Are we truly imitating Christ Jesus? Do others recognize us by the fruit we bear? Are we living lives of integrity and authenticity?

Writing this book has also helped myself because most times the message goes to the messenger first. Whether you are in leadership or not, we are all representatives of God and need to make sure that we are representing him well.

In the chapters ahead, we will delve into key aspects of our spiritual walk:

Chapter 1: The Anointing – A Gift from God

- Understanding the nature, purpose, and power of the anointing.

Chapter 2: When the Anointing Lifts

- Embracing our humanity and recognizing our identity apart from our gifts.

Chapter 3: Integrity – The Core of Our Being

- The importance of integrity and practical steps to cultivate it.

Chapter 4: Living a Life of Consistency

- Aligning our public and private lives and building a consistent character rooted in Christ.

Chapter 5: The Fruits of the Spirit – Evidence of Christ in Us

- How the fruits manifest in our lives and their impact on others.

Chapter 6: Bearing Fruit That Lasts

- Nurturing and sustaining spiritual fruit, and its importance in our witness.

Chapter 7: Knowing Who You Are in Christ

- Embracing our identity in Christ and understanding our worth.

Chapter 8: The Importance of the Five-Fold Ministry in Building the Body of Christ

- Exploring the roles within the five-fold ministry and their significance.

Chapter 9: The Importance of Character in Leadership and Beyond

- The critical role of character in leadership and everyday life.

Chapter 10: Emulating Christ Jesus

- Practical ways to follow Jesus' example and the transformation that comes from Christ-likeness.

Chapter 11: A Life of Authenticity and Purpose

- Embracing our true identity in Christ and finding purpose beyond the anointing.

Chapter 12: Iron Sharpens Iron

- The importance of accountability and mutual growth within the body of Christ.

Chapter 13: Transforming Your Mind

- The critical role of renewing our minds in our spiritual growth.

Chapter 14: Only Jesus Is the Wonder

- Keeping our focus on Jesus as the true source of our strength and identity.

Chapter 15: Putting Your Flesh Under Subjection

- Strategies for subduing the flesh and living by the Spirit, especially when the anointing lifts.

Chapter 16: The Accuser of the Brethren

- Recognizing and overcoming the tendency to judge and criticize others, fostering a spirit of unity.

Each chapter is designed to help you delve deeper into these aspects, with practical steps, biblical examples, and personal reflections. The journey of faith is not just about the extraordinary moments but also about the daily commitment to live in alignment with God's will.

As you read this book, I encourage you to reflect on your own life. Who are you when the anointing lifts? How can you cultivate a character that remains steadfast and true, no matter the season? Let this book be a guide and a companion on your path to becoming who you are called to be.

May you find joy and fulfillment in living a Christ-centered life, grounded in integrity and authenticity. And may your journey lead you to a deeper understanding of your true identity in Christ, beyond the anointing.

Blessings on your journey,

Simone Williams-Young

Acknowledgement

First and Foremost thank you to my Lord and Savior Jesus Christ for constantly loving me beyond my faults. Looking beyond the surface and always seeing the best in me.

Thank you to my husband, Sr. Elder Reuben L. Young. Not only my husband my writing coach, my encourager, my teacher, my covering, and an awesome father. I love you and appreciate you so much.

Thank you to my Pastor Chief Apostle Michael L. Rowles from the Wrecking Crew for Christ Holiness Church. Your teachings and guidance are what helped me write this book. You are always teaching your leaders about the importance of love, forgiveness, character, and integrity. You teach us how to fight in the spirit and how important it is to have a relationship with God and how to seek him for ourselves. I honor you and appreciate your leadership and thank God for you.

Thank you to my mother, Author, and Pastor Brenda J Williams. Thank you for raising me and showing me by example what it is to be a virtuous and Holy woman of God.

Prologue

Welcome to a journey of discovery, a journey that goes beyond the spiritual highs and profound experiences of feeling anointed by God. This book is about exploring a deeper question: who are we when the anointing lifts?

It's easy to admire those who move with divine grace and power, those whose gifts seem to shine brightly, drawing everyone in. But what happens when those moments fade? When the spotlight dims, who are we at our core? This book aims to uncover the essence of our true selves beyond the visible manifestations of God's power.

In these pages, we'll delve into what it means to live a life of integrity, authenticity, and consistency. We'll look at the lives of biblical figures who experienced both the anointing and the everyday realities of being human. We'll reflect on our call to imitate Christ, not just in grand gestures, but in our daily actions and decisions.

Each chapter is designed to be both a mirror and a guide. As a mirror, it will help us see where we are now in our spiritual journey. As a guide, it will provide practical steps and insights to help us grow closer to God and live out His calling for our lives.

We'll talk about the importance of bearing good fruit, staying connected to Jesus, and allowing God to prune us so we can grow even more. We'll explore the joy and challenge of living a Christ-centered life,

1

finding our true identity in Him, and embracing our purpose beyond our gifts and abilities.

This isn't just a book of theological concepts; it's a call to action. It invites us to rise above our spiritual experiences and live a life of daily surrender, intentional growth, and unwavering faith. It's about realizing that while the anointing is a precious gift, our true identity is rooted in our relationship with Jesus and our commitment to His mission.

So, as you read, I hope you feel encouraged and challenged. I hope you find practical advice and deep spiritual insights. And most importantly, I hope you come to know, with unshakable certainty, who you are when the anointing lifts.

Let's embark on this journey together, discovering the joy, fulfillment, and transformation that comes from living authentically for Christ. Welcome to the journey of becoming who you are called to be.

Introduction

~cൈ∞ഉ~

Book Guide: Journey Through "After the Anointing Lifts: Who Are You?"

Welcome to your journey through *"After the Anointing Lifts: Who Are You?"* This book is more than just a series of chapters to read; it's an interactive guide designed to help you reflect deeply on your role in the body of Christ and how to live out your faith authentically.

How to Use This Book

1. **Prepare to Engage**

Before diving into each chapter, grab a notebook and a pen. This book encourages you to not only read but also to reflect and interact with the content. The insights and questions provided are meant to prompt self-examination and spiritual growth.

2. **Read and Reflect**

Each chapter is designed to present key concepts and scriptural insights related to your journey of faith. As you read, take your time to ponder the material. Ask yourself how the teachings apply to your life, your role in the church, and your personal walk with Christ.

3. **Interactive Sections**

At the end of each chapter, you will find reflection questions and practical steps. These are not just for passive reading but are meant for active engagement. Write down your answers, thoughts, and any revelations you may have. This practice will help you internalize the content and make meaningful changes in your life.

4. **Application**

The ultimate goal is to apply what you've learned. Reflect on how the principles from each chapter can be integrated into your daily life and interactions with others. Consider how you can use your gifts and character to positively impact the body of Christ and build up the community.

5. **Encouragement, Not Condemnation**

This book is intended to be a tool for encouragement and growth, not condemnation. It aims to help you understand and embrace your identity in Christ, and to use your gifts and character for His glory. As you reflect, remember that this is a journey of personal development and spiritual maturity.

One

Chapter 1

The Anointing – A Gift from God

Understanding the Nature of the Anointing

The anointing is a divine empowerment from God that enables individuals to perform tasks and fulfill callings that would otherwise be impossible through mere human effort. Imagine you have a special talent, like being exceptionally skilled at a sport or an instrument. Now, consider that God enhances this talent with His power, making it even more extraordinary. This is the essence of the anointing—God's special grace that empowers and equips us for specific purposes.

In the bible, anointing was symbolized by pouring oil over someone's head to signify that God chose them for a particular task. This act represented God's presence and power resting on that person, granting them the ability to achieve what would be impossible on their own.

1 John 2:27 (NIV) explains:

> *"As for you, the anointing you received from him remains in you, and you do not need anyone to teach you. But as his anointing teaches you about all things and as that anointing is real, not counterfeit—just as it has taught you, remain in him."*

Biblical Examples of Anointed Individuals

David: One of the most notable examples of anointed individuals in the Bible is King David. When David was a young shepherd boy, God chose him to be the future king of Israel. The prophet Samuel poured oil over David's head, symbolizing that God's Spirit was with him. This anointing empowered David to defeat Goliath, lead Israel with wisdom, and write many of the Psalms. Despite his flaws, David's leadership and worship were marked by his divine anointing.

1 Samuel 16:13 (NIV) says:

> *"So Samuel took the horn of oil and anointed him in the presence of his brothers, and from that day on the Spirit of the Lord came powerfully upon David."*

Moses: Moses is another significant example. Anointed by God to lead the Israelites out of slavery in Egypt, Moses was empowered to perform miracles, such as parting the Red Sea and bringing water from a rock. Though he felt unqualified for such a monumental task, God's anointing equipped him to fulfill this divine mission.

Exodus 4:12 (NIV) tells us:

> *"Now go; I will help you speak and will teach you what to say."*

Jesus: The ultimate example of anointing is Jesus Christ. Anointed by the Holy Spirit, Jesus was empowered to preach good news, heal the brokenhearted, and set captives free. His entire ministry was characterized by the power of the Holy Spirit, showcasing God's love and power to the world.

Luke 4:18-19 (NIV) says:

> *"The Spirit of the Lord is on me, because he has anointed me to proclaim good news to the poor. He has sent me to proclaim freedom for the prisoners and recovery of sight for the blind, to set the oppressed free, to proclaim the year of the Lord's favor."*

Elijah and Elisha: The prophets Elijah and Elisha also exemplified the power of the anointing. Elijah performed dramatic miracles, including calling down fire from heaven (1 Kings 18:36-38), while Elisha, his successor, carried out numerous miracles, such as raising the dead (2 Kings 4:32-35). Both operated under a profound anointing that demonstrated God's authority and power.

The Apostles: After receiving the Holy Spirit at Pentecost, the apostles were anointed to boldly preach the gospel, heal the sick, and spread the message of Jesus (Acts 2). Their anointing was instrumental in the rapid growth of the early church, illustrating the power and effectiveness of operating under divine empowerment.

The Purpose and Power of the Anointing

The anointing serves several key purposes:

- **Empowerment for Ministry**: The anointing equips believers with the gifts and abilities needed to carry out God's work effectively. It enables them to preach, teach, heal, and serve with divine authority and impact.

- **Confirmation of God's Calling**: The presence of the anointing often confirms that God has chosen and set apart an individual for a specific task or ministry. It signifies God's favor and endorsement.
- **Manifestation of God's Presence**: The anointing provides a tangible demonstration of God's power. Miracles, signs, and wonders often accompany it, drawing people to faith and revealing God's presence in a powerful way.

Isaiah 61:1 (NIV) states:

> *"The Spirit of the Sovereign Lord is on me, because the Lord has anointed me to proclaim good news to the poor. He has sent me to bind up the brokenhearted, to proclaim freedom for the captives and release from darkness for the prisoners."*

The anointing can bring healing, perform miracles, provide wisdom, and inspire others. It's like a divine superpower, granted by God for specific purposes. When David faced Goliath, it was not his strength alone but God's power working through him that led to victory. This power is available to all believers who seek to align with God's will.

The Allure of Operating Under the Anointing

Operating under the anointing is profoundly fulfilling. It offers a sense of purpose, direction, and a deep connection to God. The allure of the anointing lies in experiencing God's power and presence in remarkable ways—seeing miracles, feeling divine guidance, and being part of something greater than oneself.

However, the anointing should not be pursued for personal glory or fame. It is meant to bring glory to God and serve others. When we operate under the anointing with the right intentions, we contribute significantly to God's work in the world.

Matthew 5:16 (NIV) reminds us:

"In the same way, let your light shine before others, that they may see your good deeds and glorify your Father in heaven."

When the Anointing Lifts

The anointing is not a permanent state. There are times when it lifts, and we must navigate life without its immediate influence. This period tests our true character and faith.

The Revelation of True Character: When the anointing lifts, our true nature is revealed. We may appear strong and capable under the anointing, but without it, our weaknesses and flaws become apparent. This period challenges us to continue exhibiting the fruits of the Spirit and maintaining integrity, patience, and humility.

- **Temperament and Self-Control**: James 1:19 (NIV) instructs us to be "quick to listen, slow to speak and slow to become angry," emphasizing the need for self-control. Can we manage our reactions and allow the Holy Spirit to guide us, even when the anointing is not actively present?
- **Integrity and Character**: Proverbs 10:9 (NIV) states, "Whoever walks in integrity walks securely, but whoever takes crooked paths will be found out." The lifting of the anointing often tests our true character and commitment to living righteously, revealing our actions in private.
- **Faith and Dependence on God**: Proverbs 3:5-6 (NIV) encourages us to "Trust in the Lord with all your heart and lean not on your own understanding." Our faith and dependence on God are tested

when we do not feel the anointing. Do we continue to trust in God's plan and remain steadfast in our faith?

Embracing the Process of Growth

Recognizing our true nature when the anointing lifts is an opportunity for growth. It calls us to:

- **Acknowledge Our Weaknesses**: Admitting our flaws is essential for growth. 2 Corinthians 12:9 (NIV) reminds us that God's "power is made perfect in weakness."
- **Seek Continual Transformation**: Romans 12:2 (NIV) urges us, "Do not conform to the pattern of this world, but be transformed by the renewing of your mind." Transformation is a continuous process.
- **Depend on the Holy Spirit**: Galatians 5:16 (NIV) instructs us to "walk by the Spirit." The Holy Spirit empowers us to live according to God's will, even when we do not feel anointed.
- **Develop Consistent Character**: Ephesians 4:1 (NIV) encourages us to "live a life worthy of the calling you have received." Strive to build a character that reflects Christ in all circumstances.

Reflection Questions

1. **Reflect on a time when you felt the anointing of God in your life. How did it impact your actions and decisions?**
2. **How do you respond when the anointing lifts? Are there specific areas where your true character is exposed?**
3. **In what ways can you cultivate self-control and patience, especially when you do not feel anointed?**
4. **Consider a moment when your integrity was tested. How did**

you handle it? What could you have done differently?

5. **How can you depend more on the Holy Spirit in your daily life, especially during challenging times?**

6. **What steps can you take to ensure your character is consistent, both in public and private?**

Understanding the anointing helps us recognize the unique gifts God has given us and inspires us to use them for His purposes. As we grow in our faith, seeking God's anointing, we can trust that He will empower us to achieve great things for His kingdom.

Two

Chapter 2

~⚬⚬~

When the Anointing Lifts

The Reality of Life Beyond the Anointing

L iving with the anointing can feel amazing. It's like having a direct connection to God's power and presence, enabling you to do incredible things. However, there are times when the anointing may not be as evident in our lives. This doesn't mean God has left us or that we are no longer valuable. It simply means that we're experiencing a different season, one that is just as important for our growth and faith.

Embracing Our Humanity and Imperfections

When the anointing isn't as strong, it's a reminder that we are human. We have flaws and imperfections, and that's okay. No one is perfect, and God doesn't expect us to be. He loves us as we are, with all our weaknesses. These moments can teach us to rely on Him rather than our abilities. Embracing our humanity means accepting that we will have ups and downs, and that's a normal part of life.

The Apostle Paul talked about this in 2 Corinthians 12:9-10 (NIV):

> *"But he said to me, 'My grace is sufficient for you, for my power is made perfect in weakness.' Therefore I will boast all the more gladly about my weaknesses, so that Christ's power may rest on me. That is why, for Christ's sake, I delight in weaknesses, in insults, in hardships, in persecutions, in difficulties. For when I am weak, then I am strong."*

Recognizing Our Identity Apart from Our Gifts

Our identity should not be based solely on the gifts and abilities God has given us. While it's wonderful to have talents and to be anointed, our true identity is found in being children of God. God loves us for who we are, not just for what we can do. It's important to remember that our worth comes from our relationship with God, not from our accomplishments or the roles we play.

In Galatians 3:26 (NIV), Paul writes:

> *"So in Christ Jesus you are all children of God through faith."*

And in Ephesians 2:10 (NIV), he reminds us:

"For we are God's handiwork, created in Christ Jesus to do good works, which God prepared in advance for us to do."

Think about it this way: Imagine you're really good at a sport, like basketball. You might feel great when you're playing well and winning games. But what if you get injured and can't play for a while? Does that mean you're not valuable anymore? Of course not. You are still you, with all your unique qualities and worth, even when you're not on the court. The same goes for our spiritual gifts and the anointing. We are valuable to God, with or without them.

Learning to Navigate the Quiet Seasons

Quiet seasons are times when we might not feel the anointing as strongly. These periods can be challenging, but they are also opportunities for growth. During these times, we can learn to deepen our relationship with God, strengthen our character, and build our faith.

Here are some tips for navigating the quiet seasons:

1. **Stay Connected to God**: Keep praying, reading the Bible, and seeking God's presence. Just because you don't feel the anointing as strongly doesn't mean God isn't with you. He promises to never leave us or forsake us.
2. Deuteronomy 31:6 (NIV) says:

   "Be strong and courageous. Do not be afraid or terrified because of them, for the Lord your God goes with you; he will never leave you nor forsake you."

1. **Trust in God's Timing**: Understand that God has a plan and a purpose for every season of our lives. Trust that He knows what

He's doing, even when we don't understand it.

2. Ecclesiastes 3:1 (NIV) tells us:

"There is a time for everything, and a season for every activity under the heavens."

1. **Reflect and Grow**: Use this time to reflect on your life and your relationship with God. Ask yourself questions like: How can I grow in my faith? What areas of my life need improvement? This is a great time for personal growth and development.
2. James 1:2-4 (NIV) encourages us:

"Consider it pure joy, my brothers and sisters, whenever you face trials of many kinds, because you know that the testing of your faith produces perseverance. Let perseverance finish its work so that you may be mature and complete, not lacking anything."

1. **Seek Support**: Don't be afraid to reach out to friends, family, or mentors for support and encouragement. We all need help sometimes, and it's important to lean on others when we're going through tough times.
2. Galatians 6:2 (NIV) says:

"Carry each other's burdens, and in this way you will fulfill the law of Christ."

1. **Be Patient**: Remember that quiet seasons won't last forever. God is always at work, even when we can't see it. Be patient and keep trusting Him.
2. Romans 8:28 (NIV) reassures us:

"And we know that in all things God works for the good of those who love him, who have been called according to his purpose."

Key Points to Remember

1. **Life beyond the anointing is a normal and important part of our spiritual journey.**
2. **Embracing our humanity and imperfections helps us rely more on God's grace.**
3. **Our identity is found in being children of God, not just in our gifts and abilities.**
4. **Quiet seasons are opportunities for growth and deepening our relationship with God.**

Understanding that the anointing may not always be evident helps us appreciate the different seasons of life. Each season has its purpose, and God uses them all to shape us into the people He wants us to be. By embracing our humanity, recognizing our true identity, and learning to navigate quiet seasons, we can grow closer to God and become more like Jesus in our everyday lives.

Reflection Questions

1. **Have you experienced a time when the anointing wasn't as evident in your life? How did it affect your relationship with God and others?**
2. **What are some ways you can embrace your humanity and imperfections during quiet seasons?**
3. **How can you remind yourself of your identity as a child of God, apart from your gifts and abilities?**
4. **What steps can you take to stay connected to God, trust His**

timing, and seek support during challenging times?

5. Reflect on a past trial or quiet season. How did it help you grow in your faith and character?

Three

Chapter 3

Integrity – The Core of Our Being

Defining Integrity in a Biblical Context

Integrity is a big word that might seem complicated, but it's actually quite simple. In a biblical context, integrity means being honest, trustworthy, and having strong moral principles. It's about doing the right thing, even when no one is watching. It means your actions, words, and thoughts align with God's truth and righteousness.

Proverbs 10:9 (NIV) says:

> *"Whoever walks in integrity walks securely, but whoever takes crooked paths will be found out."*

The Importance of Integrity in Our Daily Lives

Having integrity is essential in our daily lives because it builds trust and respect. When people see that you are honest and reliable, they are more likely to trust and respect you. Integrity also brings peace of mind because you know you are living according to God's will.

In our schools, friendships, and future careers, integrity will help us stand out in a positive way. It's easy to go along with what everyone else is doing, but having integrity means standing firm in what is right, even if it's hard.

Stories of Biblical Figures Who Demonstrated Integrity

1. **Joseph**: Joseph is a great example of integrity. Despite being sold into slavery by his brothers, he remained faithful to God. When Potiphar's wife tried to seduce him, Joseph refused and said, "How then could I do such a wicked thing and sin against God?" (Genesis 39:9, NIV). Even though he was falsely accused and put in prison, Joseph maintained his integrity and was eventually elevated to a position of great power in Egypt.

2. **Daniel**: Daniel is another example of integrity. When he was taken to Babylon, he resolved not to defile himself with the royal food and wine, choosing instead to follow God's dietary laws (Daniel 1:8, NIV). Later, despite a decree that made praying to anyone other than the king illegal, Daniel continued to pray to God three times a day. His integrity led him to face the lions' den, but God protected him because of his faithfulness (Daniel 6).

3. **Job**: Job is known for his unwavering integrity despite immense suffering. Even when he lost everything—his wealth, his health, and his family—he remained faithful to God and refused to curse Him. Job 2:3 (NIV) says, "And he still maintains his integrity,

19

though you incited me against him to ruin him without any reason." Job's story teaches us that true integrity means remaining faithful to God, no matter what happens.

Practical Steps to Cultivate Integrity

1. **Be Honest**: Always tell the truth, even when it's hard. Ephesians 4:25 (NIV) says, "Therefore each of you must put off falsehood and speak truthfully to your neighbor, for we are all members of one body."
2. **Keep Your Promises**: If you say you're going to do something, do it. Psalm 15:4 (NIV) praises the person "who keeps an oath even when it hurts, and does not change their mind."
3. **Be Consistent**: Let your actions match your words. James 1:22 (NIV) advises, "Do not merely listen to the word, and so deceive yourselves. Do what it says."
4. **Seek God's Guidance**: Pray and read the Bible regularly to understand God's will for your life. Psalm 119:105 (NIV) says, "Your word is a lamp for my feet, a light on my path."
5. **Surround Yourself with People of Integrity**: Spend time with friends and mentors who demonstrate integrity. Proverbs 13:20 (NIV) teaches, "Walk with the wise and become wise, for a companion of fools suffers harm."

The Impact of Integrity on Our Roles as Leaders

Integrity is especially important for leaders. People look up to leaders for guidance and example. When leaders demonstrate integrity, they build a foundation of trust and respect with those they lead. Conversely, a lack of integrity can damage relationships, harm reputations, and hinder the ability to lead effectively.

In Titus 2:7-8 (NIV), Paul instructs:

> *"In everything set them an example by doing what is good. In your teaching show integrity, seriousness and soundness of speech that cannot be condemned, so that those who oppose you may be ashamed because they have nothing bad to say about us."*

Leaders who lack integrity can cause confusion and hurt. When their actions do not align with their words, it can lead to distrust and disillusionment among followers. This not only affects the immediate relationships but also impacts the broader community, including the body of Christ.

Key Points to Remember

1. **Integrity means being honest and doing the right thing, even when no one is watching.**
2. **Integrity builds trust and respect in our daily lives.**
3. **Biblical figures like Joseph, Daniel, and Job exemplified integrity in challenging situations.**
4. **Cultivating integrity involves being honest, keeping promises, being consistent, seeking God's guidance, and surrounding ourselves with people of integrity.**
5. **Integrity is crucial for leaders, as it establishes trust and sets a positive example for others to follow.**

Integrity is at the core of who we are as followers of Christ. It's about living in a way that honors God and reflects His character. As we strive to cultivate integrity in our lives, we will not only grow closer to God but also become a positive influence on those around us. By following these practical steps and learning from the examples of biblical figures, we can develop integrity and make it a defining part of our character.

Reflection Questions

1. **What does integrity mean to you personally, and how do you see it reflected in your daily life?**
2. **Can you think of a time when showing integrity was difficult but you chose to do the right thing? What was the outcome?**
3. **How can you ensure that your actions, words, and thoughts align with God's truth and righteousness?**
4. **In what ways can you encourage and support others to cultivate integrity in their lives?**
5. **If you are in a leadership position, how can you set an example of integrity for those you lead?**

Reflecting on these questions can help you understand the importance of integrity in your own life and inspire you to live in a way that honors God and positively impacts others.

Four

Chapter 4

Living a Life of Consistency

Aligning Our Public and Private Lives

L iving a life of consistency means that who we are in private is the same as who we are in public. It means our actions, words, and thoughts align with our beliefs no matter where we are or who we are with. This kind of consistency is important because it builds trust and integrity. People can see when we are genuine and when we live out what we believe.

Matthew 6:1 (NIV) warns us:

"Be careful not to practice your righteousness in front of others to be seen by them. If you do, you will have no reward from your Father in heaven."

The Danger of Duality and Hypocrisy

Duality means living two different lives—one in public and one in private. Hypocrisy is when our actions don't match our words. Both are dangerous because they can damage our relationships with others and with God. If people see that we are not who we say we are, they will lose trust in us. More importantly, God sees our hearts and knows when we are being insincere.

Jesus spoke strongly against hypocrisy in Matthew 23:27-28 (NIV):

> *"Woe to you, teachers of the law and Pharisees, you hypocrites! You are like whitewashed tombs, which look beautiful on the outside but on the inside are full of the bones of the dead and everything unclean. In the same way, on the outside you appear to people as righteous but on the inside you are full of hypocrisy and wickedness."*

Impact on Others

When we live hypocritically, it can cause others to turn away from Christ and the church. People are watching our actions, especially when we claim to follow Jesus. If they see us saying one thing but doing another, they might think that all Christians are insincere. This can lead them to lose interest in following Christ and even to stop going to church.

Jesus also warned about causing others to stumble in their faith. In Matthew 18:6 (NIV), He says:

> *"If anyone causes one of these little ones—those who believe in me— to stumble, it would be better for them to have a large millstone hung around their neck and to be drowned in the depths of the sea."*

Jeremiah 23:1 (NIV) further emphasizes this:

"Woe to the shepherds who are destroying and scattering the sheep of my pasture!" declares the Lord.

Building a Consistent Character Rooted in Christ

Building a consistent character starts with being rooted in Christ. This means letting our relationship with Jesus shape every part of our lives. When we spend time in prayer, read the Bible, and seek to follow Jesus, our character begins to reflect His. We become more loving, patient, kind, and honest—traits that are the same whether we are at home, school, or church.

Colossians 2:6-7 (NIV) encourages us:

> *"So then, just as you received Christ Jesus as Lord, continue to live your lives in him, rooted and built up in him, strengthened in the faith as you were taught, and overflowing with thankfulness."*

Testimonies of Those Who Live Consistently

1. **Daniel**: As mentioned earlier, Daniel is a great example of living a consistent life. Despite the pressures of living in a foreign land, he remained faithful to God. He prayed regularly, followed God's laws, and didn't compromise his beliefs. This consistency not only saved him in the lions' den but also influenced the king and those around him.
2. Daniel 6:10 (NIV) shows his consistency:

> *"Now when Daniel learned that the decree had been published, he went home to his upstairs room where the windows opened toward Jerusalem. Three times a day he got down on his knees and prayed, giving thanks to his God, just as he had done before."*

1. **Ruth**: Ruth is another example of consistency. After the death of her husband, she chose to stay with her mother-in-law Naomi and adopt her faith. Ruth's consistency in her loyalty and faithfulness was evident in her actions. She worked hard to provide for Naomi and followed God's ways. Her consistent character eventually led to her becoming the great-grandmother of King David.
2. Ruth 1:16 (NIV) shows her commitment:

"But Ruth replied, 'Don't urge me to leave you or to turn back from you. Where you go I will go, and where you stay I will stay. Your people will be my people and your God my God.'"

Chapter Review and Reflection Questions

Chapter Review

1. **Consistency**: Aligning our public and private lives to reflect our beliefs.
2. **Danger of Duality**: Living differently in public and private leads to hypocrisy.
3. **Impact on Others**: Hypocrisy can cause others to turn away from Christ and the church.
4. **Rooted in Christ**: Building character through a strong relationship with Jesus.
5. **Testimonies**: Learning from biblical examples like Daniel and Ruth who lived consistently.

Reflection Questions

1. **What are some areas in your life where you feel you are not consistent?**

2. Why is it important to align your public and private lives?
3. How can spending time with God help you build a consistent character?
4. Can you think of a person in your life who lives consistently? What can you learn from them?
5. How can you apply the lessons from Daniel and Ruth's lives to your own life?
6. Have you ever seen someone's hypocrisy cause others to turn away from Christ or the church? How did that affect you?
7. What steps can you take to ensure your actions don't lead others away from Christ?

Living a life of consistency is challenging but incredibly rewarding. When our lives align with our beliefs, we build trust, integrity, and a strong relationship with God. By learning from biblical examples and focusing on our relationship with Christ, we can develop a consistent character that honors God and positively impacts those around us.

Five

Chapter 5

❦

The Fruits of the Spirit – Evidence of Christ in Us

Exploring Galatians 5:22-23

The Fruits of the Spirit are qualities that grow in our lives when we follow Jesus and allow the Holy Spirit to work in us. These fruits are listed in Galatians 5:22-23 (NIV):

> *"But the fruit of the Spirit is love, joy, peace, forbearance, kindness, goodness, faithfulness, gentleness and self-control. Against such things there is no law."*

These qualities show others that we belong to Christ and are living in a way that pleases God. Just like how healthy trees produce good fruit, our lives should produce good qualities that reflect Jesus.

How the Fruits of the Spirit Manifest in Our Lives

1. **Love**: This is a selfless, sacrificial, and unconditional care for others. When we love, we put others' needs before our own and show them God's love through our actions.
2. **Joy**: Joy is a deep sense of happiness and contentment that comes from knowing God. It's not based on circumstances but on our relationship with Him.
3. **Peace**: Peace means being calm and trusting God, even in difficult situations. It's about having confidence that God is in control.
4. **Forbearance (Patience)**: Patience is the ability to wait without getting angry or upset. It's about showing grace and understanding to others, even when it's hard.
5. **Kindness**: Kindness is being considerate, helpful, and caring toward others. It involves doing good deeds and speaking gently.
6. **Goodness**: Goodness is living in a way that is morally right and reflects God's character. It means being honest, fair, and upright.
7. **Faithfulness**: Faithfulness is being reliable and trustworthy. It's about keeping our promises and being loyal to God and others.
8. **Gentleness**: Gentleness means being humble and caring in our interactions with others. It's about being sensitive and compassionate.
9. **Self-control**: Self-control is the ability to control our desires and impulses. It means making wise choices and resisting temptation.

Personal Reflections and Growth in Each Fruit

- **Love**: Reflect on how you can show love to your family, friends, and even those who are hard to love. Acts of kindness and forgiveness are great ways to demonstrate love.
- **Joy**: Think about the things that bring you joy in your relationship

with God. Maybe it's reading the Bible, praying, or singing worship songs. Focus on these to deepen your joy.

- **Peace**: When you feel stressed or worried, remember to pray and trust God. Take deep breaths and remind yourself that God is in control.
- **Patience**: Practice being patient in your daily life. Whether you're waiting in line or dealing with a difficult person, take a deep breath and choose to respond with grace.
- **Kindness**: Look for opportunities to be kind. It could be a smile, a kind word, or helping someone in need. Small acts of kindness can make a big difference.
- **Goodness**: Commit to doing what is right, even when it's hard. Stand up for what you believe in and be honest in all your dealings.
- **Faithfulness**: Be dependable in your commitments. If you say you will do something, follow through. Be loyal to your friends and family.
- **Gentleness**: Speak and act with gentleness. Be considerate of others' feelings and show compassion.
- **Self-control**: Practice self-control by setting boundaries for yourself. Whether it's with food, social media, or other activities, make wise choices that honor God.

Encouraging Others to Recognize the Fruits in Their Lives

When we live out the Fruits of the Spirit, people see God in us. They notice our love, joy, peace, patience, kindness, goodness, faithfulness, gentleness, and self-control, and it makes them curious about what makes us different. This opens up opportunities to share about our faith and what Jesus has done in our lives.

Matthew 5:16 (NIV) says:

"In the same way, let your light shine before others, that they may see your good deeds and glorify your Father in heaven."

When others see the Fruits of the Spirit in us, it can inspire them to want to know more about Jesus. It's important to encourage others by recognizing and affirming the fruits you see in their lives. This can help them grow in their faith and desire to follow Christ more closely.

Chapter Review and Reflection Questions

Chapter Review

1. **Fruits of the Spirit**: Qualities that grow in our lives when we follow Jesus and allow the Holy Spirit to work in us (Galatians 5:22-23).
2. **Manifestation**: Love, joy, peace, patience, kindness, goodness, faithfulness, gentleness, and self-control should be evident in our lives.
3. **Personal Growth**: Reflect and work on each fruit in your daily life to become more like Christ.
4. **Impact on Others**: Living out these fruits can lead others to see God in us and want to know more about Him.

Reflection Questions

1. **Which Fruit of the Spirit do you see most in your life? Which one do you need to work on the most?**
2. **How can you show love to someone who is difficult to love?**
3. **What are some ways you can cultivate joy and peace in your life, even during tough times?**
4. **Think of a time when you had to be patient. How did it make**

you feel, and what can you learn from that experience?

5. **Describe a recent act of kindness you performed or received. How did it impact you or others?**

6. **What steps can you take to practice more self-control in your daily life?**

7. **How can you encourage others to recognize and grow the Fruits of the Spirit in their lives?**

By living out the Fruits of the Spirit, we not only grow closer to God but also become a beacon of His love and grace to those around us. As we reflect on these fruits and work to cultivate them in our lives, we can make a positive impact on our world and inspire others to seek a relationship with Jesus.

Six

Chapter 6

⚬⚬⚬

Bearing Fruit That Lasts

The Importance of Bearing Good Fruit

Bearing good fruit is essential for every believer. It's a sign of our relationship with Christ and the work of the Holy Spirit in us. When we bear good fruit, we show the world that we belong to Jesus. Good fruit includes love, kindness, patience, and other qualities that reflect Christ's character.

Matthew 7:16-17 (NIV) says:

> *"By their fruit you will recognize them. Do people pick grapes from thornbushes, or figs from thistles? Likewise, every good tree bears good fruit, but a bad tree bears bad fruit."*

Our actions and behaviors are the fruit that people see. If our lives produce good fruit, it demonstrates our faith and the impact Jesus has on us. Conversely, if we bear bad fruit, it can harm our witness and turn others away from God.

Jesus' Teachings on Fruitfulness (John 15)

Jesus taught extensively about bearing fruit in John 15. He used the metaphor of a vine and branches to illustrate our relationship with Him and the importance of staying connected to Him.

John 15:1-4 (NIV) says:

> *"I am the true vine, and my Father is the gardener. He cuts off every branch in me that bears no fruit, while every branch that does bear fruit he prunes so that it will be even more fruitful. You are already clean because of the word I have spoken to you. Remain in me, as I also remain in you. No branch can bear fruit by itself; it must remain in the vine. Neither can you bear fruit unless you remain in me."*

Jesus emphasizes that we must remain in Him to bear fruit. Without a strong connection to Jesus, we cannot produce the qualities that reflect His character. God, the gardener, prunes us to help us become more fruitful. This process can be challenging, but it helps us grow and bear even more fruit.

John 15:5 (NIV) continues:

> *"I am the vine; you are the branches. If you remain in me and I in you, you will bear much fruit; apart from me you can do nothing."*

How to Nurture and Sustain Spiritual Fruit

1. **Remain in Christ**: Stay connected to Jesus through prayer, reading the Bible, and worship. This relationship is the foundation of bearing good fruit.
2. **Allow God to Prune You**: Be open to God's correction and guidance. Pruning can be uncomfortable, but it is necessary for growth and increased fruitfulness.
3. **Cultivate the Fruits of the Spirit**: Actively work on developing the Fruits of the Spirit in your life. Reflect on each fruit and find ways to practice them daily.
4. **Seek the Holy Spirit's Help**: The Holy Spirit empowers us to bear fruit. Ask the Holy Spirit to fill you and guide you in your daily walk.
5. **Be Patient**: Bearing fruit takes time. Be patient with yourself and trust that God is at work in you, even when you don't see immediate results.
6. **Stay Accountable**: Surround yourself with other believers who can encourage you and help you grow. Accountability helps keep you on track and motivated.

Impacting Others Through the Fruit We Bear

When we bear good fruit, it impacts those around us. Our lives become a testimony to God's love and power. People see the difference in us and are drawn to know more about Jesus.

Matthew 5:16 (NIV) says:

> *"In the same way, let your light shine before others, that they may see your good deeds and glorify your Father in heaven."*

Here are a few ways our fruit can impact others:

1. **Inspiring Others**: When people see our love, patience, and kindness, they are inspired to seek the same qualities in their lives. Our example can lead them to Jesus.
2. **Building Trust**: Consistent good fruit builds trust with others. They know they can rely on us, which opens doors for deeper relationships and conversations about faith.
3. **Encouraging Growth**: Our fruit can encourage fellow believers to grow in their faith. When we share our experiences and how God is working in us, it motivates others to pursue their own spiritual growth.
4. **Making a Difference**: Good fruit can make a tangible difference in our communities. Acts of kindness, service, and love reflect God's kingdom on earth and meet real needs.

Chapter Review and Reflection Questions

Chapter Review

1. **Importance of Good Fruit**: Good fruit reflects our relationship with Christ and impacts our witness.
2. **Jesus' Teachings on Fruitfulness**: Staying connected to Jesus is essential for bearing fruit (John 15).
3. **Nurturing Spiritual Fruit**: Remain in Christ, allow God to prune you, cultivate the Fruits of the Spirit, seek the Holy Spirit's help, be patient, and stay accountable.
4. **Impacting Others**: Our fruit inspires, builds trust, encourages growth, and makes a difference.

Reflection Questions

1. What kind of fruit are you currently bearing in your life? Is it good or bad?
2. How can you stay more connected to Jesus to ensure you bear good fruit?
3. What are some areas in your life where you need God's pruning? How can you be open to this process?
4. How can you actively cultivate the Fruits of the Spirit in your daily life?
5. Think of a time when someone else's good fruit impacted you. How did it influence your faith or actions?
6. In what ways can you let your light shine to those around you, so they may see your good deeds and glorify God?

By focusing on bearing fruit that lasts, we not only grow closer to God but also make a significant impact on the world around us. As we nurture and sustain our spiritual fruit, others will see God in us and be drawn to Him, ultimately leading to a greater witness for Christ and His kingdom.

Seven

Chapter 7

⤜⤛⤚⤙

Knowing Who You Are in Christ

Understanding Your Identity in Christ

K nowing who you are in Christ is crucial for living a fulfilling and effective Christian life. Our identity in Christ shapes how we see ourselves and how we interact with others. When we understand our identity, we use our gifts and roles to build up the body of Christ rather than tearing others down.

In 2 Corinthians 5:17 (NIV), the Apostle Paul writes:

"Therefore, if anyone is in Christ, the new creation has come: The old has gone, the new is here!"

This verse emphasizes that being in Christ means we are new creations. Our old self with its flaws and sins is gone, and we are transformed into someone new. This transformation gives us a new identity and purpose. Understanding this identity helps us to use our gifts wisely and compassionately.

Using Your Gifts to Build, Not to Tear Down

Every believer has been given unique gifts by God, whether it's teaching, leadership, service, or another role. However, these gifts are not meant to elevate ourselves or to be used against others. Instead, they are given to build up the body of Christ and to serve others.

1 Corinthians 12:4-7 (NIV) states:

> *"There are different kinds of gifts, but the same Spirit distributes them. There are different kinds of service, but the same Lord. There are different kinds of working, but in all of them and in everyone it is the same God at work. Now to each one the manifestation of the Spirit is given for the common good."*

This passage reminds us that our gifts are for the common good, not for personal gain or to harm others. We are called to use our gifts to support and encourage others in their faith journey.

The Danger of Misusing Gifts

When we don't understand our identity in Christ, there's a risk of misusing our gifts. We might use our roles or talents to criticize, belittle, or compete with others. This behavior can cause division and harm within the church.

James 3:16 (NIV) warns:

> *"For where you have envy and selfish ambition, there you find*

disorder and every evil practice."

Misusing our gifts due to envy or selfish ambition can lead to conflict and disorder. Instead of fostering unity, it can drive people apart and create a toxic environment.

Embracing Your Role in Building Up the Body of Christ

1. **Serve Others with Love**: Use your gifts to serve and uplift others. Whether it's through acts of kindness, encouragement, or sharing wisdom, let love be your guiding principle.

Ephesians 4:15-16 (NIV) says:

> *"Instead, speaking the truth in love, we will grow to become in every respect the mature body of him who is the head, that is, Christ. From him the whole body, joined and held together by every supporting ligament, grows and builds itself up in love, as each part does its work."*

1. **Celebrate Others' Gifts**: Recognize and celebrate the gifts and contributions of others. Acknowledging and supporting the roles of fellow believers fosters a healthy and collaborative environment.
2. **Seek Humility**: Approach your gifts with humility. Remember that all abilities come from God and are meant to serve others, not ourselves.

Philippians 2:3 (NIV) advises:

> *"Do nothing out of selfish ambition or vain conceit. Rather, in humility value others above yourselves."*

1. **Encourage Growth**: Use your gifts to encourage others in their spiritual growth. Be a mentor, a supporter, and a source of inspiration.

Chapter Review and Reflection Questions

Chapter Review

1. **Identity in Christ**: Understanding our identity as new creations in Christ helps us use our gifts properly (2 Corinthians 5:17).
2. **Purpose of Gifts**: Gifts are meant to build up the body of Christ, not to harm others (1 Corinthians 12:4-7).
3. **Danger of Misuse**: Using gifts for selfish reasons can lead to division and conflict (James 3:16).
4. **Building Up the Body**: Serve others with love, celebrate their gifts, seek humility, and encourage growth (Ephesians 4:15-16, Philippians 2:3).

Reflection Questions

1. **How does understanding your identity in Christ affect how you use your gifts?**
2. **In what ways can you use your gifts to build up and support others rather than tearing them down?**
3. **Have you ever seen a gift or role being misused in a way that caused harm? How did that impact you or the community?**
4. **How can you celebrate and support the gifts of others in your church or community?**
5. **What steps can you take to ensure you use your gifts with humility and love?**
6. **Think about a time when someone used their gifts to encour-**

    age and uplift you. How did it affect your faith or perspective?

7. **What are some practical ways you can use your gifts to encourage growth in others and contribute to the body of Christ?**

Understanding who you are in Christ transforms how you use your gifts and interact with others. By recognizing your new identity and focusing on building up the body of Christ, you contribute to a supportive and loving community. This approach not only honors God but also reflects His love and grace to those around you.

Eight

Chapter 8

~❦~

The Importance of the Five-Fold Ministry in Building the Body of Christ

Understanding the Five-Fold Ministry

T he Five-Fold Ministry is a key concept in understanding how God equips the church to grow and thrive. This ministry framework is outlined in Ephesians 4:11-13 (NIV):

> *"So Christ himself gave the apostles, the prophets, the evangelists, the pastors and teachers, to equip his people for works of service, so that the body of Christ may be built up until we all reach unity in the faith and in the knowledge of the Son of God and become mature, attaining to the whole measure of the fullness of Christ."*

Each role in the Five-Fold Ministry—apostles, prophets, evangelists, pastors, and teachers—has a unique purpose in equipping and building up the church. These roles work together to ensure that the body of Christ grows in faith, unity, and maturity.

The Role of Each Office

1. **Apostles**: Apostles are leaders who establish and oversee churches and ministries. They lay foundational principles and guide the overall direction of the church. Their role is crucial in setting up structures and networks that support church growth.
2. **Scripture Reference**: Acts 2:42 (NIV) – "They devoted themselves to the apostles' teaching and to fellowship, to the breaking of bread and to prayer."
3. **Prophets**: Prophets provide guidance and insight into God's will, often speaking on behalf of God to the church. They offer direction and encouragement, helping the church stay aligned with God's plans.
4. **Scripture Reference**: 1 Corinthians 14:3 (NIV) – "But the one who prophesies speaks to people for their strengthening, encouraging and comfort."
5. **Evangelists**: Evangelists focus on spreading the message of Jesus and bringing others to faith. They are passionate about sharing the gospel and expanding the reach of the church.
6. **Scripture Reference**: 2 Timothy 4:5 (NIV) – "But you, keep your head in all situations, endure hardship, do the work of an evangelist, discharge all the duties of your ministry."
7. **Pastors**: Pastors care for and shepherd the congregation. They provide spiritual guidance, counsel, and support to help individuals grow in their faith and overcome challenges.
8. **Scripture Reference**: 1 Peter 5:2 (NIV) – "Be shepherds of God's

flock that is under your care, watching over them—not because you must, but because you are willing, as God wants you to be; not pursuing dishonest gain, but eager to serve."

9. **Teachers**: Teachers explain and apply biblical truths, helping believers understand and live out their faith. They play a critical role in educating and discipling the church.

10. **Scripture Reference**: James 3:1 (NIV) – "Not many of you should become teachers, my fellow believers, because you know that we who teach will be judged more strictly."

Tying It to "After the Anointing Lifts—Who Are You?"

The Five-Fold Ministry is vital in building up the body of Christ, especially after the initial excitement of anointing or spiritual experiences fades. When the anointing lifts, the true measure of our character and our contribution to the church is revealed. It's not just about the dramatic moments of divine empowerment but about our consistent, everyday efforts to serve and build the body of Christ.

After the anointing lifts, who we are in Christ and how we contribute to the church's growth become evident. The Five-Fold Ministry helps us understand our roles and responsibilities in the body of Christ, ensuring that we are not merely relying on spiritual highs but actively working to support and develop others.

The Importance of Using Gifts Wisely

When we understand our role within the Five-Fold Ministry, we can use our gifts more effectively. We avoid using our roles to dominate or belittle others and instead use them to build up and encourage. Each role supports and complements the others, creating a balanced and effective ministry that reflects Christ's love and purpose.

1 Corinthians 12:12-14 (NIV) emphasizes this:

> *"Just as a body, though one, has many parts, but all its many parts form one body, so it is with Christ. For we were all baptized by one Spirit so as to form one body—whether Jews or Gentiles, neither slave nor free—and we were all given the one Spirit to drink. Even so the body is not made up of one part but of many."*

Chapter Review and Reflection Questions

Chapter Review

1. **Five-Fold Ministry**: The Five-Fold Ministry includes apostles, prophets, evangelists, pastors, and teachers, each with a unique role in building up the body of Christ (Ephesians 4:11-13).
2. **Role of Each Office**: Each role contributes to the growth and maturity of the church by providing guidance, spreading the gospel, caring for the flock, and teaching biblical truths.
3. **After the Anointing Lifts**: True character and contributions are revealed after initial spiritual experiences. The Five-Fold Ministry helps us stay focused on building the church.
4. **Using Gifts Wisely**: Understanding our role within the Five-Fold Ministry helps us use our gifts to serve and support others rather than for personal gain or to harm.

Reflection Questions

1. **Which role in the Five-Fold Ministry resonates with you the most? Why?**
2. **How can you use your gifts and role to build up the body of Christ rather than to elevate yourself?**

3. **Reflect on a time when the anointing or spiritual experience seemed to fade. How did you respond, and what did you learn about your role in the church?**
4. **In what ways can you contribute to the growth and unity of the church through your specific gifts and role?**
5. **How can you support and collaborate with others who have different roles within the Five-Fold Ministry?**
6. **What practical steps can you take to ensure that you are using your gifts to serve others and not for personal gain?**

Understanding the Five-Fold Ministry helps us recognize the value of each role in building up the body of Christ. It also encourages us to use our gifts wisely and to focus on serving others, reflecting Christ's love and purpose. By embracing our roles and contributing to the church's growth, we honor God and strengthen the community of believers.

Nine

Chapter 9

⸙

The Importance of Character in Leadership and Beyond

Understanding the Role of Character

C haracter is the essence of who we are, especially when no one is watching. It encompasses our values, integrity, and the consistency of our actions. For leaders and believers alike, character is crucial because it affects how we interact with others, how we lead, and ultimately how we represent Christ.

In Proverbs 27:19 (NIV), we read:

"As water reflects the face, so one's life reflects the heart."

Our character reflects what's in our hearts and how we handle different situations. It's not just about how we act when things are going well, but how we respond in challenging circumstances. This consistency in our character builds trust and credibility.

The Impact of Good Character

Good character is foundational for effective leadership and impactful living. It inspires trust, fosters respect, and builds strong, healthy relationships. Leaders with good character set a positive example for others and create an environment where people feel valued and supported.

1 Timothy 4:12 (NIV) provides guidance on the importance of character in leadership:

> *"Don't let anyone look down on you because you are young, but set an example for the believers in speech, in conduct, in love, in faith, and in purity."*

Leaders are called to set an example in all aspects of their lives. Good character influences how they speak, act, and lead, setting a standard for others to follow. It's about living in a way that reflects Christ's love and integrity.

The Consequences of Bad Character

Conversely, bad character can have detrimental effects on individuals and communities. It can lead to broken trust, damaged relationships, and hinder the growth of the church. Bad character undermines the message of Christ and can cause others to question the faith.

In Matthew 7:15-16 (NIV), Jesus warns:

"Watch out for false prophets. They come to you in sheep's clothing, but inwardly they are ferocious wolves. By their fruit you will recognize them."

This passage highlights the importance of authentic character. False prophets may appear righteous on the outside but have corrupt character on the inside. Their actions and words reveal their true nature and can mislead others.

The Power of Words

Words are a powerful reflection of our character. They can build up or tear down, offer encouragement or spread negativity. For both leaders and believers, the way we communicate can significantly impact our effectiveness and the way we are perceived.

James 3:5-6 (NIV) underscores the impact of our words:

"Likewise, the tongue is a small part of the body, but it makes great boasts. Consider what a great forest is set on fire by a small spark. The tongue also is a fire, a world of evil among the parts of the body. It corrupts the whole body, sets the whole course of one's life on fire, and is itself set on fire by hell."

Our words can influence and shape our lives and the lives of others. Leaders, in particular, must be careful with their words, ensuring they are aligned with their character and reflect the love and truth of Christ.

Cultivating Good Character

1. **Self-Examination**: Regularly assess your character and seek feedback from others. Be honest about areas that need growth and work on them intentionally.
2. **Accountability**: Surround yourself with trusted mentors or accountability partners who can offer guidance and help you stay on track.
3. **Prayer and Reflection**: Seek God's help in developing your character. Pray for wisdom, strength, and the ability to reflect Christ's character in all you do.
4. **Consistency**: Strive for consistency between your public and private life. Let your actions and words align with your values and beliefs.
5. **Learning and Growth**: Read Scripture, engage in personal development, and learn from others who exhibit strong character.

Chapter Review and Reflection Questions

Chapter Review

1. **Importance of Character**: Character reflects who we are and influences our leadership and interactions (Proverbs 27:19).
2. **Impact of Good Character**: Good character builds trust, fosters respect, and sets a positive example (1 Timothy 4:12).
3. **Consequences of Bad Character**: Bad character can lead to broken trust and damage the message of Christ (Matthew 7:15-16).
4. **Power of Words**: Words reflect our character and can have a profound impact on others (James 3:5-6).
5. **Cultivating Good Character**: Self-examination, accountability, prayer, consistency, and growth are key to developing strong

character.

Reflection Questions

1. **What aspects of your character reflect Christ's love and integrity? What areas need improvement?**
2. **How can you set an example in your speech and conduct to positively influence those around you?**
3. **Recall a time when someone's bad character affected you or others. How did it impact you, and what did you learn from it?**
4. **How can you be more mindful of the impact of your words on others?**
5. **What steps can you take to cultivate and maintain good character in your daily life?**
6. **Think about a leader or role model whose character you admire. What qualities do they exhibit, and how can you incorporate those into your own life?**
7. **How can regular self-examination and accountability contribute to your personal growth and effectiveness as a leader?**

Character is fundamental to how we live out our faith and lead others. By developing good character and being mindful of the impact of our words, we reflect Christ more accurately and create a positive influence in our communities. Whether as leaders or believers, our character speaks volumes about our faith and can either draw others to Christ or push them away.

Ten

Chapter 10

❧

Emulating Christ Jesus

The Call to Imitate Christ

As believers, we are called to imitate Christ in every aspect of our lives. This call is a profound one, urging us to reflect the character, love, and holiness of Jesus in our daily actions and interactions. The Apostle Paul emphasizes this call in his letter to the Ephesians.

Ephesians 5:1-2 (NIV) says:

> *"Follow God's example, therefore, as dearly loved children and walk in the way of love, just as Christ loved us and gave himself up for us as a fragrant offering and sacrifice to God."*

This passage highlights two key aspects of imitating Christ: following

God's example and walking in love. Christ's love was sacrificial and selfless, serving as the ultimate model for how we should live our lives.

Practical Ways to Follow Jesus' Example

1. **Love Unconditionally**: Jesus loved without conditions, showing compassion and grace to everyone He encountered. We can follow His example by loving others, regardless of their backgrounds or actions.
2. John 13:34-35 (NIV) says:

   "A new command I give you: Love one another. As I have loved you, so you must love one another. By this everyone will know that you are my disciples if you love one another."

1. Reflect on how you can show unconditional love in your daily interactions. Consider ways to extend grace and kindness, even to those who may be difficult to love.
2. **Serve Others Selflessly**: Jesus demonstrated servant leadership, humbling Himself to serve others. We are called to serve those around us with humility and a willing heart.
3. Mark 10:45 (NIV) says:

   "For even the Son of Man did not come to be served, but to serve, and to give his life as a ransom for many."

1. Look for opportunities to serve in your community, church, or family. Serving others not only blesses them but also helps us grow in Christ-like humility and compassion.
2. **Forgive Freely**: Jesus forgave those who wronged Him, even as He hung on the cross. Forgiveness is a powerful act that reflects

Christ's love and mercy.

3. Luke 23:34 (NIV) says:

"Jesus said, 'Father, forgive them, for they do not know what they are doing.'"

1. Examine your heart for any unforgiveness or bitterness. Pray for the strength to forgive, knowing that forgiveness brings healing and freedom.
2. **Live Righteously**: Jesus lived a sinless life, fully obedient to God's will. While we are not perfect, we can strive to live righteously by following God's commandments and seeking His guidance.
3. 1 Peter 2:21-22 (NIV) says:

"To this you were called, because Christ suffered for you, leaving you an example, that you should follow in his steps. 'He committed no sin, and no deceit was found in his mouth.'"

1. Reflect on areas where you can align your life more closely with God's word. Seek His help to overcome temptations and live in obedience.
2. **Seek God's Will**: Jesus sought the Father's will in everything He did. We are called to seek God's will through prayer, Bible study, and a heart of surrender.
3. Matthew 26:39 (NIV) says:

"Going a little farther, he fell with his face to the ground and prayed, 'My Father, if it is possible, may this cup be taken from me. Yet not as I will, but as you will.'"

1. Develop a habit of seeking God's guidance in your decisions and

daily life. Trust that His will is perfect and seek to align your desires with His.

Stories of Individuals Who Emulate Christ

1. **Mother Teresa**: Known for her selfless service to the poor and sick in Calcutta, Mother Teresa embodied Christ's love and compassion. Her life was a testament to sacrificial love and unwavering faith.
2. **Corrie ten Boom**: During World War II, Corrie ten Boom and her family hid Jews from the Nazis, risking their own lives. After the war, she spoke about forgiveness and reconciliation, reflecting Christ's grace and mercy.
3. **Dietrich Bonhoeffer**: A German pastor and theologian, Bonhoeffer stood against the Nazi regime and was ultimately martyred for his faith. His writings on discipleship and his steadfast commitment to following Christ's example inspire believers to this day.

The Transformation That Comes from Christ-likeness

Emulating Christ leads to profound personal and spiritual transformation. As we strive to imitate Jesus, we become more like Him in character and action, experiencing the fruits of the Spirit in our lives.
2 Corinthians 3:18 (NIV) says:

> *"And we all, who with unveiled faces contemplate the Lord's glory, are being transformed into his image with ever-increasing glory, which comes from the Lord, who is the Spirit."*

This transformation is a continuous process that shapes us into the image of Christ, bringing us closer to God and enabling us to reflect

His love and righteousness to the world.

Chapter Review and Reflection Questions

Chapter Review

1. **Call to Imitate Christ**: We are called to follow Christ's example of love and sacrifice (Ephesians 5:1-2).
2. **Practical Ways to Follow Jesus' Example**: Love unconditionally, serve selflessly, forgive freely, live righteously, and seek God's will.
3. **Stories of Individuals Who Emulate Christ**: Mother Teresa, Corrie ten Boom, and Dietrich Bonhoeffer are examples of living Christ-like lives.
4. **Transformation Through Christ-likeness**: Emulating Christ leads to personal and spiritual transformation, bringing us closer to God.

Reflection Questions

1. **In what areas of your life do you feel called to imitate Christ more closely?**

- Reflect on specific aspects of Jesus' character that you want to develop in your own life.

1. **How can you show unconditional love to those around you?**

- Consider practical ways to extend Christ's love and grace to others.

1. **What opportunities do you have to serve others selflessly?**

- Identify ways you can serve in your community, church, or family.

1. **Is there anyone you need to forgive? How can you take steps toward forgiveness?**

- Pray for the strength to forgive and take practical steps to reconcile.

1. **In what ways can you seek to live more righteously?**

- Examine areas where you can align more closely with God's word and seek His guidance.

1. **How can you develop a habit of seeking God's will daily?**

- Consider incorporating prayer, Bible study, and surrender into your daily routine.

By striving to emulate Christ, we grow in our faith and become living testimonies of His love and grace. Our transformed lives can inspire others and draw them closer to God, fulfilling our call to be His disciples and reflect His light to the world.

Eleven

Chapter 11

A Life of Authenticity and Purpose

Embracing Our True Identity in Christ

U nderstanding and embracing our true identity in Christ is foundational to living a life of authenticity and purpose. When we recognize that our worth and identity come from being children of God, we can live confidently and authentically.

2 Corinthians 5:17 (NIV) says:

> *"Therefore, if anyone is in Christ, the new creation has come: The old has gone, the new is here!"*

This verse reminds us that, in Christ, we are made new. Our past mistakes and failures no longer define us. Instead, we are defined by our relationship with Jesus and the transformation He brings.

Galatians 2:20 (NIV) says:

> *"I have been crucified with Christ and I no longer live, but Christ lives in me. The life I now live in the body, I live by faith in the Son of God, who loved me and gave himself for me."*

When we embrace our identity in Christ, we understand that our lives are no longer our own. We live for Him, allowing His love and purpose to guide us.

Living Authentically Before God and Others

Living authentically means being genuine and transparent about who we are. It involves honesty about our struggles, weaknesses, and imperfections while also celebrating the unique gifts and strengths God has given us.

Psalm 139:13-14 (NIV) says:

> *"For you created my inmost being; you knit me together in my mother's womb. I praise you because I am fearfully and wonderfully made; your works are wonderful, I know that full well."*

God knows us intimately and loves us completely. We don't need to hide our true selves from Him or others. Instead, we can live authentically, trusting that God's love covers all our flaws and empowers us to grow.

James 5:16 (NIV) says:

> *"Therefore confess your sins to each other and pray for each other so that you may be healed. The prayer of a righteous person is powerful and effective."*

Being open and honest with others about our struggles fosters a sense of community and accountability. It allows us to support one another and grow together in our faith.

Finding Purpose Beyond the Anointing

Our purpose in life goes beyond any specific anointing or spiritual gift we may have. While these gifts are important, our ultimate purpose is to know God and make Him known.

Jeremiah 29:11 (NIV) says:

> *"'For I know the plans I have for you,' declares the Lord, 'plans to prosper you and not to harm you, plans to give you hope and a future.'"*

God has a unique plan and purpose for each of our lives. When we seek His will and follow His guidance, we can live out that purpose with confidence and joy.

Matthew 28:19-20 (NIV) says:

> *"Therefore go and make disciples of all nations, baptizing them in the name of the Father and of the Son and of the Holy Spirit, and teaching them to obey everything I have commanded you. And surely I am with you always, to the very end of the age."*

Our mission is to share the love of Christ with others and to make disciples. This purpose transcends any specific anointing and is the foundation of our calling as believers.

Encouragement for the Journey Ahead

Living a life of authenticity and purpose is a journey that requires perseverance and faith. We will face challenges and obstacles, but God promises to be with us every step of the way.

Isaiah 41:10 (NIV) says:

> *"So do not fear, for I am with you; do not be dismayed, for I am your God. I will strengthen you and help you; I will uphold you with my righteous right hand."*

We can take comfort in knowing that God is our constant companion and source of strength. He will guide us, uphold us, and give us the courage to live authentically and purposefully.

Philippians 1:6 (NIV) says:

> *"Being confident of this, that he who began a good work in you will carry it on to completion until the day of Christ Jesus."*

God is faithful to complete the work He has started in us. As we trust in Him and remain steadfast in our faith, we will see His purposes unfold in our lives.

Chapter Review and Reflection Questions

Chapter Review

1. **Embracing Our True Identity in Christ**: Our worth and identity come from being children of God, not our past mistakes or failures.
2. **Living Authentically Before God and Others**: Authenticity involves being genuine and transparent, trusting that God's love

covers our flaws.

3. **Finding Purpose Beyond the Anointing**: Our ultimate purpose is to know God and make Him known, beyond any specific spiritual gifts.

4. **Encouragement for the Journey Ahead**: God promises to be with us, guide us, and complete the work He has started in us.

Reflection Questions

1. **How can you embrace your true identity in Christ more fully?**

- Reflect on any past mistakes or failures that you need to release to embrace the new creation you are in Christ.

1. **What does living authentically before God and others look like for you?**

- Consider ways you can be more genuine and transparent in your relationships.

1. **How can you find and pursue your purpose beyond your specific anointing or spiritual gifts?**

- Think about how you can live out the Great Commission and share Christ's love with others.

1. **What encouragement do you need for the journey ahead?**

- Identify specific promises from God's Word that you can hold onto during challenging times.

1. **How can you support others in their journey toward authenticity and purpose?**

- Consider ways to encourage and uplift fellow believers as they seek to live authentically and purposefully.

By embracing our true identity in Christ, living authentically, finding our purpose beyond specific gifts, and relying on God's encouragement, we can live a life of authenticity and purpose that honors God and impacts the world around us.

Twelve

Chapter 12

~ ⚬⚬⚬ ~

Iron Sharpens Iron

T he Biblical Principle of Mutual Encouragement
Proverbs 27:17 (NIV) says:

"As iron sharpens iron, so one person sharpens another."

The concept of iron sharpening iron is a powerful metaphor for the importance of fellowship and mutual encouragement among believers. It emphasizes that we are meant to grow and strengthen each other through our interactions, relationships, and shared experiences. Just as iron blades become sharper when they rub against each other, we too become more refined and equipped for God's work when we engage with one another in meaningful and spiritually enriching ways.

The Importance of Godly Relationships

Godly relationships play a crucial role in our spiritual growth and development. They provide us with accountability, support, and encouragement. When we surround ourselves with fellow believers who are committed to living according to God's principles, we create an environment where we can grow in integrity, character, and faith.

Ecclesiastes 4:9-10 (NIV) states:

> *"Two are better than one, because they have a good return for their labor: If either of them falls down, one can help the other up. But pity anyone who falls and has no one to help them up."*

Practical Ways to Sharpen Each Other

1. **Accountability Partners**: Find a trusted friend or mentor who can hold you accountable in your walk with Christ. Share your struggles, successes, and goals with each other, and pray for one another regularly.
2. **Bible Study Groups**: Join or form a small group that meets regularly to study the Bible. Discussing God's Word together helps deepen your understanding and application of biblical principles.
3. **Prayer Partners**: Partner with someone who will pray with and for you consistently. Praying together strengthens your bond and brings you closer to God.
4. **Service Projects**: Engage in service projects with other believers. Working together to serve others not only blesses those in need but also strengthens your faith and unity.
5. **Encouragement and Exhortation**: Make it a habit to encourage and exhort one another. Share words of affirmation, scripture, and positive feedback to build each other up.

Hebrews 10:24-25 (NIV) reminds us:

"And let us consider how we may spur one another on toward love and good deeds, not giving up meeting together, as some are in the habit of doing, but encouraging one another—and all the more as you see the Day approaching."

Stories of Iron Sharpening Iron

1. **Paul and Timothy**: Paul mentored Timothy, providing guidance, encouragement, and accountability. Their relationship is a model of how experienced believers can help younger ones grow in faith and ministry (1 Timothy 1:2, 2 Timothy 1:2).
2. **Ruth and Naomi**: Ruth's loyalty to Naomi and their mutual support exemplify how godly relationships can strengthen and sustain us during difficult times (Ruth 1:16-17).
3. **David and Jonathan**: Their deep friendship and mutual encouragement showcase the power of supportive, God-centered relationships (1 Samuel 18:1-4).

Thirteen

Chapter 13

❧❦❧

Transforming Your Mind

The Importance of a Renewed Mind
Transformation in the Christian life begins with the renewal of our minds. Our thoughts shape our actions, attitudes, and ultimately our character. To live a life that honors God, we must align our thinking with His Word and His ways.

Romans 12:2 (NIV) captures this transformation process:

> *"Do not conform to the pattern of this world, but be transformed by the renewing of your mind. Then you will be able to test and approve what God's will is—his good, pleasing and perfect will."*

Renewing our minds involves a conscious effort to reject worldly perspectives and embrace God's truth. It is an ongoing process that requires dedication and a willingness to change.

Steps to Transforming Your Mind

1. **Immerse Yourself in Scripture**: Regularly reading and meditating on the Bible helps us understand God's character and His will for our lives. Scripture provides the foundation for a renewed mind.
2. **Psalm 119:11 (NIV)** says:

   "I have hidden your word in my heart that I might not sin against you."

1. **Pray for Wisdom and Understanding**: Ask God to give you wisdom and insight as you study His Word. Prayer opens our hearts and minds to the Holy Spirit's guidance.
2. **James 1:5 (NIV)** encourages us:

   "If any of you lacks wisdom, you should ask God, who gives generously to all without finding fault, and it will be given to you."

1. **Guard Your Thoughts**: Be mindful of what you allow into your mind through media, conversations, and other influences. Focus on things that are pure, noble, and praiseworthy.
2. **Philippians 4:8 (NIV)** instructs:

   "Finally, brothers and sisters, whatever is true, whatever is noble, whatever is right, whatever is pure, whatever is lovely, whatever is admirable—if anything is excellent or praiseworthy—think about such things."

1. **Practice Gratitude and Positivity**: Cultivating a thankful heart

and a positive outlook helps reframe our thinking in line with God's promises and faithfulness.

2. **1 Thessalonians 5:18 (NIV)** says:

"Give thanks in all circumstances; for this is God's will for you in Christ Jesus."

1. **Seek Godly Counsel**: Surround yourself with mentors and friends who can offer wisdom and encouragement. They can help you stay accountable in your journey of mind renewal.
2. **Proverbs 15:22 (NIV)** notes:

"Plans fail for lack of counsel, but with many advisers they succeed."

The Impact of a Renewed Mind

A renewed mind leads to a transformed life. It changes how we view ourselves, others, and our circumstances. When our thoughts align with God's truth, we are better equipped to live out His will and experience His peace and joy.

Colossians 3:2 (NIV) urges us:

"Set your minds on things above, not on earthly things."

Reflection Questions

1. **What steps can you take to immerse yourself more deeply in Scripture?**
2. **How can you incorporate prayer for wisdom and understanding into your daily routine?**
3. **What influences in your life do you need to guard against to protect your mind?**

4. In what ways can you practice gratitude and positivity to transform your thinking?
5. Who in your life can offer godly counsel and support in your journey of mind renewal?

Fourteen

Chapter 14

~⚬⚬⚬~

Only Jesus Is the Wonder

Recognizing Jesus as the Ultimate Source of Wonder
In our spiritual journey, it's essential to recognize that only Jesus is the true source of wonder. While the anointing and spiritual gifts are significant, they are secondary to the person of Jesus Christ. Our focus should always be on Him and His work in our lives. **Hebrews 12:2 (NIV)** emphasizes this point:

> *"Fixing our eyes on Jesus, the pioneer and perfecter of faith. For the joy set before him he endured the cross, scorning its shame, and sat down at the right hand of the throne of God."*

Jesus is the author and finisher of our faith. He is the one who sustains us and brings us into the fullness of life with God. All wonder and awe should be directed towards Him.

The Centrality of Christ in Our Lives

1. **Jesus as the Foundation**: Our faith is built on the foundation of Jesus Christ. He is the cornerstone upon which everything else is constructed.
2. **1 Corinthians 3:11 (NIV)** declares:

   "For no one can lay any foundation other than the one already laid, which is Jesus Christ."

1. **Jesus as the Sustainer**: Jesus not only initiates our faith but also sustains it. He is with us through every season, providing strength and guidance.
2. **Colossians 1:17 (NIV)** explains:

   "He is before all things, and in him all things hold together."

1. **Jesus as the Goal**: Our ultimate goal is to become more like Christ. He is the standard and the example we strive to follow.
2. **Philippians 3:10 (NIV)** says:

   "I want to know Christ—yes, to know the power of his resurrection and participation in his sufferings, becoming like him in his death."

Living in Awe of Jesus

1. **Worship**: Regularly spend time in worship, reflecting on who Jesus is and what He has done. Worship helps keep our focus on Him and cultivates a heart of gratitude and reverence.
2. **John 4:24 (NIV)** reminds us:

"God is spirit, and his worshipers must worship in the Spirit and in truth."

1. **Study His Life**: Delve into the Gospels to learn more about Jesus' life, teachings, and miracles. Studying His life inspires us to live more like Him.
2. **Matthew 11:29 (NIV)** invites us:

"Take my yoke upon you and learn from me, for I am gentle and humble in heart, and you will find rest for your souls."

1. **Share His Love**: Demonstrate Christ's love to others through acts of kindness and compassion. Sharing His love magnifies the wonder of who He is.
2. **1 John 4:19 (NIV)** states:

"We love because he first loved us."

1. **Anticipate His Return**: Keep the hope of Jesus' return at the forefront of your mind. This anticipation fuels our faith and encourages us to live with purpose and urgency.
2. **Titus 2:13 (NIV)** speaks of our blessed hope:

"While we wait for the blessed hope—the appearing of the glory of our great God and Savior, Jesus Christ."

Reflection Questions

1. **How can you make Jesus the foundation of your daily life?**
2. **In what ways do you need to rely more on Jesus as your sustainer?**

3. What steps can you take to know Jesus more deeply and become more like Him?
4. How can you incorporate regular worship into your routine to keep your focus on Jesus?
5. Who in your life needs to experience the love of Jesus through your actions?

Fifteen

Chapter 15

Putting Your Flesh Under Subjection

Understanding the Battle with the Flesh

Living a life that honors God involves a constant battle with our flesh—our sinful nature that is prone to desires and actions contrary to God's will. The Apostle Paul vividly describes this struggle in Romans 7:18-19 (NIV):

> *"For I have the desire to do what is good, but I cannot carry it out. For I do not do the good I want to do, but the evil I do not want to do—this I keep on doing."*

Our flesh can be stubborn and persistent, leading us into habits and behaviors that distance us from God. However, by recognizing this battle and relying on the power of the Holy Spirit, we can put our flesh under subjection and live lives that reflect Christ's character. This is particularly important when the anointing lifts, and we must rely on our foundational character and relationship with God.

Biblical Mandate for Subjection

The Bible consistently calls us to put our flesh under subjection and live according to the Spirit. Paul writes in Galatians 5:16-17 (NIV):

> *"So I say, walk by the Spirit, and you will not gratify the desires of the flesh. For the flesh desires what is contrary to the Spirit, and the Spirit what is contrary to the flesh. They are in conflict with each other, so that you are not to do whatever you want."*

This passage highlights the necessity of walking by the Spirit to overcome the desires of the flesh. It's not a one-time event but a daily commitment to surrender our will to God's. When the anointing lifts, and we no longer feel the supernatural empowerment, our commitment to subduing the flesh and walking in the Spirit becomes even more critical.

Practical Steps to Subdue the Flesh

1. **Daily Surrender**: Begin each day by surrendering your desires and will to God. Pray for the Holy Spirit to guide and strengthen you throughout the day. Romans 12:1 (NIV) encourages us:

> *"Therefore, I urge you, brothers and sisters, in view of God's mercy, to offer your bodies as a living sacrifice, holy and pleasing to God— this is your true and proper worship."*

1. **Renew Your Mind**: Transform your thinking by immersing yourself in God's Word. Romans 12:2 (NIV) instructs:

> *"Do not conform to the pattern of this world, but be transformed*

by the renewing of your mind. Then you will be able to test and approve what God's will is—his good, pleasing and perfect will."

1. **Avoid Temptation**: Identify areas of weakness and avoid situations that may lead to temptation. 1 Corinthians 10:13 (NIV) offers assurance:

"No temptation has overtaken you except what is common to mankind. And God is faithful; he will not let you be tempted beyond what you can bear. But when you are tempted, he will also provide a way out so that you can endure it."

1. **Control Your Temper**: One of the most challenging aspects of putting the flesh under subjection is controlling our temper and being slow to speak. James 1:19-20 (NIV) advises:

"My dear brothers and sisters, take note of this: Everyone should be quick to listen, slow to speak and slow to become angry, because human anger does not produce the righteousness that God desires."

1. When we allow the Holy Spirit to lead us, we are better equipped to respond with patience and grace rather than reacting impulsively.
2. **Rely on the Holy Spirit**: Trust the Holy Spirit to guide you in what to do and say, especially in challenging situations. John 14:26 (NIV) promises:

"But the Advocate, the Holy Spirit, whom the Father will send in my name, will teach you all things and will remind you of everything I have said to you."

1. **Accountability**: Surround yourself with believers who will hold

you accountable and encourage you in your walk with Christ. James 5:16 (NIV) emphasizes the power of community:

"Therefore confess your sins to each other and pray for each other so that you may be healed. The prayer of a righteous person is powerful and effective."

1. **Engage in Spiritual Disciplines**: Regularly practice spiritual disciplines such as prayer, fasting, worship, and Bible study. These disciplines help strengthen your spirit and weaken the grip of the flesh.

Biblical Examples of Subjection

1. **Jesus**: Jesus is the ultimate example of putting the flesh under subjection. Despite facing intense temptation in the wilderness, He resisted and relied on Scripture to overcome the devil's schemes (Matthew 4:1-11). His life exemplified total submission to the Father's will, even to the point of death on the cross (Philippians 2:8).
2. **Paul**: The Apostle Paul was transparent about his struggles with the flesh, yet he consistently chose to walk by the Spirit. In 1 Corinthians 9:27 (NIV), he writes:

"No, I strike a blow to my body and make it my slave so that after I have preached to others, I myself will not be disqualified for the prize."

1. **Joseph**: Joseph's integrity and commitment to God enabled him to resist Potiphar's wife's advances. He fled from temptation, choosing to honor God rather than gratify his fleshly desires

(Genesis 39:6-12).

The Role of the Holy Spirit

The Holy Spirit is essential in our journey to subdue the flesh. Galatians 5:22-23 (NIV) describes the fruits of the Spirit:

"But the fruit of the Spirit is love, joy, peace, forbearance, kindness, goodness, faithfulness, gentleness and self-control. Against such things there is no law."

These fruits are evidence of a life lived under the Spirit's control. By inviting the Holy Spirit to fill us daily, we can produce these fruits and overcome the desires of the flesh. This daily filling is crucial when the anointing lifts, and we rely more heavily on the Spirit's work in our character.

Living Differently from the World

As followers of Christ, we are called to respond differently than the world does. This includes our reactions to conflict, stress, and temptation. Romans 12:17-18 (NIV) instructs:

"Do not repay anyone evil for evil. Be careful to do what is right in the eyes of everyone. If it is possible, as far as it depends on you, live at peace with everyone."

By allowing the Holy Spirit to guide our responses, we can demonstrate Christ's love and patience even in difficult situations, showing the world a different way of living.

Reflection Questions

1. What areas of your life are most susceptible to the desires of the flesh?

2. How can you implement daily surrender and renewal of your mind to combat these desires?
3. Who can you ask to hold you accountable in your journey to subdue the flesh?
4. What spiritual disciplines can you incorporate into your routine to strengthen your spirit?
5. Reflect on a time when you successfully resisted temptation. What strategies did you use, and how can you apply them consistently?
6. How can you practice being slow to speak and controlling your temper in your daily interactions?
7. In what ways can you rely more on the Holy Spirit to guide your words and actions?

Putting our flesh under subjection is a continuous process that requires dedication, humility, and reliance on the Holy Spirit. By following these biblical principles and practical steps, we can live lives that honor God and reflect His character, even when the anointing lifts. As we die to ourselves daily, we grow closer to God and become more like Christ, embodying His love and grace in all we do. This process reveals our true identity and character, beyond the powerful moments of anointing, and roots us firmly in who we are in Christ.

4o

Sixteen

Chapter 16

∽◌⁹◌◌⁹◌∽

The Accuser of the Brethren

Understanding the Role of the Accuser
Revelation 12:10 (NIV) says:

> *"For the accuser of our brothers and sisters, who accuses them before our God day and night, has been hurled down."*

Satan is referred to as the accuser of the brethren. He seeks to sow discord, doubt, and condemnation among believers. His goal is to divide and weaken the body of Christ by turning us against each other and against ourselves. Understanding his tactics is crucial to standing firm in our identity and unity in Christ.

The Dangers of Accusation

Accusation can be incredibly destructive within the body of Christ. It undermines trust, damages relationships, and hinders spiritual growth.

When we allow ourselves to become tools of accusation, we align with Satan's purpose rather than God's.

James 4:11-12 (NIV) warns:

> *"Brothers and sisters, do not slander one another. Anyone who speaks against a brother or sister or judges them speaks against the law and judges it. When you judge the law, you are not keeping it, but sitting in judgment on it. There is only one Lawgiver and Judge, the one who is able to save and destroy. But you—who are you to judge your neighbor?"*

Overcoming the Accuser's Tactics

1. **Recognize and Reject Accusation**: Be aware of the enemy's tactics and refuse to participate in gossip, slander, or judgment against others. Instead, choose to speak words of life and encouragement.
2. **Forgive and Seek Forgiveness**: Unforgiveness fuels the accuser's agenda. Choose to forgive others and seek forgiveness when you have wronged someone. This breaks the cycle of accusation and promotes healing and unity.
3. **Stand Firm in Your Identity**: Remember who you are in Christ. The enemy's accusations cannot change your identity as a beloved child of God. Stand firm in the truth of God's Word and reject any lies or accusations that come your way.
4. **Support and Encourage One Another**: Instead of tearing each other down, commit to building each other up. Encourage your fellow believers, pray for them, and support them in their walk with Christ.

1 Thessalonians 5:11 (NIV) instructs:

"Therefore encourage one another and build each other up, just as in fact you are doing."

Stories of Overcoming Accusation

1. **Job**: Job faced intense accusations from his friends during his time of suffering. Despite their harsh words, Job remained steadfast in his faith and integrity, ultimately being vindicated by God (Job 42:7-9).
2. **Jesus and the Adulterous Woman**: When the Pharisees brought a woman caught in adultery to Jesus, He responded with grace and wisdom, refusing to condemn her and instead offering forgiveness and a call to repentance (John 8:1-11).
3. **Paul**: The Apostle Paul faced many false accusations throughout his ministry. He consistently responded with integrity, grace, and unwavering commitment to the gospel, demonstrating how to overcome accusation with faith and perseverance (Acts 24:10-21).

Tying It All Together

When we understand the importance of mutual encouragement and the destructive nature of accusation, we can better navigate our identity beyond the anointing. By sharpening each other and rejecting the enemy's accusations, we align ourselves with God's purposes and grow in integrity and Christ-likeness. We are called to be a supportive, encouraging community that reflects the love and unity of Christ, standing firm against the tactics of the accuser and building each other up in faith.

Reflection Questions

1. How can you be more intentional about encouraging and sharpening the believers around you?
2. Are there any relationships in your life that need mending due to accusations or misunderstandings? How can you take steps toward reconciliation?
3. How can you stand firm against the enemy's accusations in your own life and the lives of others?
4. Reflect on a time when someone else's encouragement helped you grow in your faith. How can you pay it forward?
5. In what ways can you cultivate a supportive and encouraging community within your church or small group?

Seventeen

Conclusion

Becoming Who We Are Called to Be

Reaffirming Our Commitment to Integrity and Authenticity

As we conclude our exploration of integrity and authenticity, it's crucial to reaffirm our commitment to these principles in our daily lives. Integrity is not a mere checklist but a lifestyle that reflects our alignment with God's truth and righteousness. Authenticity goes hand-in-hand with integrity, ensuring that our outward actions and inner convictions are in harmony.

In Proverbs 4:25-27 (NIV), we read:

> *"Let your eyes look straight ahead; fix your gaze directly before you. Give careful thought to the paths for your feet and be steadfast in all your ways. Do not turn to the right or the left; keep your foot from evil."*

This passage encourages us to remain steadfast in our commitment to integrity. By keeping our focus on God's path, we ensure that our actions and character remain aligned with His will.

Reaffirming our commitment means regularly evaluating our lives to ensure that we are living according to the principles of integrity and authenticity. It involves being honest with ourselves, seeking God's guidance, and making necessary adjustments to align our lives with His standards.

The Joy and Fulfillment of Living a Christ-Centered Life

Living a Christ-centered life brings unparalleled joy and fulfillment. When we place Christ at the center of our lives, our actions, decisions, and relationships reflect His love and purpose. This alignment with God's will brings a deep sense of peace and contentment.

John 10:10 (NIV) reminds us of the abundant life that Christ offers:

> "The thief comes only to steal and kill and destroy; I have come that they may have life, and have it to the full."

A Christ-centered life is not about living in perfection but about experiencing the fullness of life that comes from a genuine relationship with Jesus. It's about finding joy in our identity as His children and fulfillment in living out His purpose for us.

Galatians 5:22-23 (NIV) describes the fruit of a life led by the Spirit:

> "But the fruit of the Spirit is love, joy, peace, forbearance, kindness, goodness, faithfulness, gentleness and self-control. Against such things there is no law."

When we live in alignment with Christ, we naturally bear the fruit of the

Spirit, which brings joy and fulfillment into our lives. Our relationships become more loving, our actions more kind, and our inner peace more profound.

A Prayer for Continued Growth and Alignment with God's Will

Heavenly Father,

We come before You with hearts full of gratitude and commitment. Thank You for guiding us through this journey of understanding integrity, authenticity, and purpose. We recognize that living a Christ-centered life requires daily dedication and alignment with Your will.

Lord, help us to reaffirm our commitment to integrity and authenticity. May our actions and thoughts consistently reflect Your truth and righteousness. Teach us to remain steadfast in our pursuit of holiness, keeping our eyes fixed on You.

Grant us the joy and fulfillment that comes from living a life centered on Christ. Fill us with the fruit of the Spirit, and let Your love, peace, and joy overflow in our lives. Help us to be a reflection of Your grace and truth in all that we do.

We pray for Your continued guidance and growth in our lives. Align our hearts with Your will, and empower us to live out our purpose with courage and faithfulness. May our lives be a testimony to Your goodness and a beacon of hope to those around us.

In Jesus' name, we pray,

Amen.

Final Thoughts: After the Anointing Lifts – Who Are You?

As we wrap up this exploration, it's essential to reflect on a crucial question: After the anointing lifts, who are you? The anointing, a powerful and transformative experience, is a gift from God that empowers us to fulfill His purposes. But what happens when its visible impact fades, and we're left in a quieter, more ordinary season of life?

The true measure of who we are is not solely defined by the anointing or its absence. It's about our core identity and how we live out our faith when the extraordinary moments give way to everyday routines. Our worth and purpose remain deeply rooted in our relationship with Christ, not in the dramatic experiences or visible signs of God's power.

Who we are is defined by our unwavering commitment to integrity, our pursuit of authenticity, and our steadfast identity as children of God. Even when the anointing is not as evident, these core aspects remain. Our integrity is a reflection of our alignment with God's truth, and our authenticity reveals the genuine nature of our relationship with Him.

In these quieter seasons, we have the opportunity to deepen our understanding of who we are in Christ. We are not diminished by the absence of the anointing but rather invited to grow in character, strength, and faithfulness. Our identity is grounded in Christ's love and His calling on our lives, which persists beyond the visible manifestations of His power.

As you move forward, remember that your true identity is anchored in Christ. Embrace the everyday moments with the same commitment to integrity and authenticity that you displayed during the times of anointing. Continue to live out your faith with purpose, knowing that every season—whether marked by visible signs or quiet faithfulness—holds value and contributes to your growth in Christ.

May you find reassurance and strength in the knowledge that you are always held in God's love, and your identity remains secure in Him. Embrace who you are called to be, regardless of the visible signs, and trust that God is working in and through you in every season of life.

References

All Scriptures are taken from Bible Gateway
  NIV
  KJV

About the Author

Prophet Simone Williams-Young can be described as a Dream and Vision encourager. She is a book publisher, entrepreneur, prophet, mentor, author, wife, grandmother, and most importantly servant of the Most High God. Her goal is to inspire people to reach towards everything that God has in store for them. She believes that no matter what happened in the past as long as God allows us to see a new day there is always a chance to do better and be better.

Simone Williams-Young is the CEO and founder of Young at Heart Publishing LLC, which was birthed to empower individuals who have a voice and a story to tell and share it with the world. Young at Heart LLC. provides every opportunity to accomplish their dreams. Simone Williams-Young is not only a successful author but also a mentor for aspiring writers. She has helped many people turn their ideas into books, guiding them through the process of planning, drafting, and publishing. She offers coaching services for anyone who wants to learn how to write and publish their books. Some of the books she has mentored include *"The Purpose Formula: Uncover Your Life's Mission and Live with Passion"* and *"The Power of Purpose: How Personal Growth Leads to Leadership"* by

Reuben L. Young. *"The Path to Success: Unlocking Your Minds Full Potential"* by James Hewitt, *"Breakdown to Breakthrough"* by Brenda J. Williams. Simone has worked on diverse types of writing projects, ranging from fiction to non-fiction, sci-fi to romance, Christian fiction, and more.

She is excited to share more of her work with you through Young at Heart Publishing LLC. Stay tuned for some amazing releases coming soon.

Simone Williams-Young is a woman of many talents and passions. She is the owner and founder of She Uniq LLC, a hair boutique that offers a variety of services and products to enhance the beauty and uniqueness of women around the world. She believes that women have different ways and forms of expressing their beauty and she wants to help them achieve their goals.

She is also the author of a book titled "I Choose to Live: Pushing through the grieving process". This book is a personal testimony of how she overcame the loss of her son, who was killed in his prime to gun violence. She authored this book to inspire and empower others who are going through grief and to show them that they can survive and thrive. She also mentors and coaches other grieving individuals who need support and guidance to move forward.

Simone Williams-Young has been featured on Daughter of the King Television Network several times and she is a board member of Heart 2 Heart Ministries International Foundation Non-Profit, a charitable organization led by Dr. Angela Roberson. She participates in various projects and initiatives that aim to help the community and spread the love of God.

Simone Williams-Young is a faithful Wrecking Crew for Christ Holiness Church member, where Chief Apostle Michael L. Rowles is the leader. She has learned a lot from his teachings and examples about leadership, service, holiness, and love. She strives to live a life that pleases God and blesses others.

You can connect with me on:

🌐 https://linktr.ee/SimoneWilliamsYoung

f https://www.facebook.com/AuthorSimoneWilliamsYoung

Also by Simone Williams Young

The library of books written by Simone Williams-Young is a range of self-help books, journals, and words of encouragement. Check out some of my releases.

I Choose to Live: Pushing Past the Grieving Process
I Choose to Live is a testament and guide on how to push through the grieving process. This book is designed to motivate and help your mindset if you have ever struggled or are currently struggling with grief. Losing someone close to you can be devastating; the goal of this book is to let you know that you are not alone and for you to strive to choose to live.

Stronger, Better, Wiser: Walk Into the New You
Stronger, Better, Wiser: Walk into the New You is a collaborative book by six authors who share their personal experiences of overcoming challenges and transforming their lives. Each chapter offers practical insights and inspiring lessons on how to tap into your inner strength, cultivate a positive mindset, and achieve your goals. Whether you are facing a career change, a health issue, a relationship problem, or any other obstacle, this book will help you discover the power of resilience and the joy of living authentically. While walking into the new you, you will also learn how to embrace your uniqueness, celebrate your achievements, and create a lasting impact on the world around you. This book is more than just a collection of stories; it is a guide to living with courage, confidence, and compassion.

www.ingramcontent.com/pod-product-compliance
Lightning Source LLC
Chambersburg PA
CBHW070728130626
46553CB00005B/2199